THE
ITALIAN
RENAISSANCE

To Richard,
my personal Renaissance man

*G*rateful acknowledgment is made to Daniela Bleichmar
of the History Department at Princeton University, Princeton,
New Jersey, for her generous assistance in reading the manuscript.

Extracts are reprinted from the following sources: page 9, *The Decameron of Giovanni Boccaccio,* translated by John Payne, published by Walter J. Black, 1972; page 18, *History of Italy and History of Florence* by Francesco Guicciardini, translated by Cecil Grayson, published by Washington Square Press, 1964; page 29, *The Notebooks of Leonardo da Vinci,* Volume 1, edited by Jean Paul Richter, published by Dover Publications, 1972; page 33, "A Complaint by Night of the Lover Not Beloved" by Francesco Petrarca, translated by Henry Howard, Earl of Surrey, and page 65, "A Carnival Song" by Lorenzo de' Medici, reprinted in *The Portable Renaissance Reader,* edited by James Bruce Ross and Mary Martin McLaughlin, published by Penguin Books, 1981; page 45, *La semplicità ingannata: Tirannia paterna* by Arcangela Tarabotti, in *Donne e società nel Seicento,* edited by Ginevra Conti Oderisio, published by Bulzoni, 1979, reprinted in *Women of the Renaissance* by Margaret L. King, published by University of Chicago Press, 1991; page 48, *Reformation Writings of Martin Luther,* translated by Bertram Lee Woolf, published by the Philosophical Library, 1953, reprinted in *The Renaissance Reader,* edited by Kenneth J. Atchity, published by HarperCollins, 1996; page 52, *Letter to Posterity* by Francesco Petrarca, in *Letters from Petrarch,* translated by Morris Bishop, published by Indiana University Press, 1966, reprinted in *The Renaissance Reader,* edited by Kenneth J. Atchity, published by HarperCollins, 1996; pages 58–59, *The Prince* by Niccolò Macchiavelli, translated by W. K. Marriott, published by Alfred A. Knopf, 1992.

CULTURES
OF THE PAST

THE
ITALIAN
RENAISSANCE

VIRGINIA SCHOMP

BENCHMARK BOOKS

MARSHALL CAVENDISH
NEW YORK

Benchmark Books
Marshall Cavendish
99 White Plains Road
Tarrytown, New York 10591-9001

www.marshallcavendish.com

© Marshall Cavendish Corporation 2003

Library of Congress Cataloging-in-Publication Data
Schomp, Virginia.
    The Italian Renaissance / by Virginia Schomp.
        p.   cm.— (Cultures of the past)
    Summary: Discusses how and why the Renaissance began in Italy, the cultural
and intellectual achievements of the Italian Renaissance, and the lasting effects
of these achievements on Western civilization. Includes bibliographical refer-
ences and index.
    ISBN 0-7614-1492-4
    1. Renaissance—Italy—Juvenile literature.   2. Italy—Civilization—1268–
1559—Juvenile literature. [1. Renaissance—Italy. 2. Italy—Civilization 1268–
1559.] I. Title. II. Series.
DG445 .S36   2003
945'.05—dc21   2002001971

Printed in Hong Kong
1 3 5 6 4 2

Book design by Carol Matsuyama
Art research by Rose Corbett Gordon, Mystic CT.

Front cover: A close-up look at the head of *David,* by Italian Renaissance artist
    Michelangelo Buonarroti
Back cover: A portrait of a noblewoman of Renaissance Florence, by Domenico
    Ghirlandaio

Photo Credits
Front cover: Galleria dell'Accademia, Florence/Bridgeman Art Library; back cover:
Thyssen-Bornemisza Collection, Madrid/Bridgeman Art Library; pages 7, 12–13,16,
30, 32, 36, 41, 43, 44, 51, 52, 64: Scala/Art Resource, NY; page 11: Santo Spirito,
Florence/Bridgeman Art Library; page 14: Archivo del Stato, Siena/Bridgeman Art
Library; page 15: Thyssen-Bornemisza Collection, Madrid/Bridgeman Art Library;
page 18: Palazzo Medici-Riccardi, Florence/Bridgeman Art Library; page 19: Museo
di San Marco dell'Angelico, Florence/Bridgeman Art Library; page 22–23: Scrovegni
(Arena) Chapel, Padua/Bridgeman Art Library; pages 24, 39, 69, Galleria degli Uffizi,
Florence/Bridgeman Art Library; page: 25: Baptistry, Florence/Bridgeman Art Library;
pages 27, 71: Duomo, Florence/Bridgeman Art Library; page 28: Louvre, Paris/Bridge-
man Art Library; page 31: Duke of Sutherland Collection, National Gallery of
Scotland/Bridgeman Art Library; page 47: Piccolomini Library, Duomo, Siena/
Bridgeman Art Library; page 54: The Art Archive; page 56: Biblioteca Trivulziana,
Milan/Bridgeman Art Library; page 59: Palazzo Vecchio (Palazzo della Signoria),
Florence/Bridgeman Art Library; page 61: Erich Lessing/Art Resource, NY; pages 62,
67: Corbis; page 70: Palazzo Pitti, Florence/Bridgeman Art Library.

CONTENTS

CHAPTER ONE

BIRTHPLACE OF THE RENAISSANCE

$\mathcal{S}$omething exciting happened in Italy in the early 1300s. To one scholar of the times, it seemed "as if on a given signal, splendid talents [were] stirring." People began looking at the world in a new way, and over the next three centuries their ideas would transform society, politics, religion, and the arts. Today historians call this cultural period the Renaissance, from the French word for "rebirth." The people of the Renaissance reached back in time to give a new birth to ancient knowledge and art forms, then developed them to glorious new heights.

Renaissance Roots

In ancient times, the Greeks and then the Romans ruled vast empires. At its height in the second century C.E.,* the Roman Empire controlled most of Europe and parts of the Middle East and northern Africa. The ancient Greeks and Romans studied the world around them and wrote important texts on science, government, and law. Their writers, artists, and architects created brilliant plays, poetry, paintings, sculptures, temples, and monuments. But in 476, the last Roman emperor was overthrown. The long period of European history known as the Middle Ages, or the medieval period, began.

During the Middle Ages, most of Europe was divided into small kingdoms and estates. Italy was not the united country we know today.

---

*Many systems of dating have been used by different cultures throughout history. This series of books uses B.C.E. (Before Common Era) and C.E. (Common Era) instead of B.C. (Before Christ) and A.D. (Anno Domini) out of respect for the diversity of the world's peoples.

Instead, the Italian peninsula was a collection of separate territories, each with its own laws, government, culture, and dialect (form of spoken language). These territories were a tempting target for foreign invaders. Seated at the southern tip of Europe, jutting out into the Mediterranean Sea, the Italian peninsula was a natural trade link between northern Europe and the cities of Africa and Asia. Throughout the Middle Ages, a parade of would-be conquerors marched through Italy, including the Byzantines, Arabs, Lombards and Franks (Germanic peoples), Normans (from France), and the Holy Roman Empire (a German-ruled alliance attempting to reunite the lands of the ancient Roman Empire). For a time, each of these powers ruled different parts of Italy, but none ever managed to win control of the entire peninsula.

By the mid-1200s, several of Italy's cities had become powers themselves. As they grew in strength and wealth, these city-states took over the lands surrounding them. The biggest and most prosperous city-states were in the north. Venice, Genoa, Pisa,

The School of Athens *by Raphael shows the ancient Greek philosophers Plato and Aristotle* (center) *surrounded by some of the Renaissance artists and scholars they would inspire centuries after their time. The artist portrayed several notable figures of Renaissance Italy in the painting: Plato* (pointing up) *looks like Leonardo da Vinci, the dark-haired man leaning on his elbow* (bottom center) *resembles Michelangelo, and Raphael himself* (the second figure to the right of Michelangelo) *gazes out at viewers.*

THE "NOT-SO-DARK" AGES

Until recently, many historians viewed the nearly one-thousand-year period between the fall of Rome and the beginning of the Renaissance as a time of ignorance and superstition, when the light of ancient Greece and Rome nearly went out. Today we know that the Middle Ages weren't quite so dark. Although much of the knowledge of the ancients was forgotten in many parts of Europe, it was never truly lost. Ancient texts were copied by Catholic monks and nuns in monasteries and convents, and preserved in Islamic libraries in northern Africa and the Middle East. Medieval writers, philosophers, artists, architects, and inventors produced their own important works. Today most historians prefer to think of the Middle Ages as a period of gradual social, political, and cultural changes, with its own vitality and creative spirit.

and other northern coastal cities were centers of trade, their busy ports bursting with activity. Ships set sail for the East carrying cloth, wool, furs, copper, and iron; others returned laden with luxuries including gold, ivory, silk, jewels, carpets, spices, and slaves. Further inland, Florence thrived on trade, manufacturing, and banking. Toward the end of the Middle Ages, more than twenty Italian city-states had populations of 20,000 or more, and Florence—home to nearly 100,000—was one of the largest cities in Europe.

Troubles and Triumphs

The fourteenth century was a troubled and dangerous time in Italy. Beginning in 1339, thousands of people starved in four separate famines, brought on by drought and poor farming practices. Between 1347 and 1351, the Black Death—a deadly plague carried by rats and fleas— spread from the East through Italy's port cities and on through the rest of Europe. An estimated two-fifths of all Europeans died in the catastrophe, including more than half the population of Italy.

Adding to the death toll were nearly constant violence and war. Throughout the century, the Italian city-states battled one another for land, wealth, and power. Larger city-states gobbled up their neighbors, until five major powers dominated the peninsula: Florence, Rome, Venice, Milan, and Naples. Mercenaries roamed the countryside between battles, looting towns and attacking travelers.

Amazingly, in the midst of all this suffering and strife, the Renaissance blossomed. Why was Italy the birthplace of the Renaissance? One reason was its location. Seated on the crossroads between West and East,

THE BLACK DEATH

In 1353, Giovanni Boccaccio described the devastations of the Black Death in Florence. A poet and storyteller, Boccaccio was one of the great writers of the early Italian Renaissance. This passage is from the *Decameron*, a collection of one hundred lively, often humorous tales set against the dark backdrop of the plague:

In men and women alike there appeared, at the beginning of the malady, certain swellings, either on the groin or under the armpits, whereof some waxed of the bigness of a common apple, others like unto an egg, some more and some less, and these the vulgar named plague-boils. . . . After awhile, the fashion of the contagion began to change into black or livid [reddish] blotches, which showed themselves in many on the arms and about the thighs and every other part of the person. . . . Not only did few recover thereof, but well nigh all died within the third day from the appearance of the aforesaid signs, this sooner and that later. . . . This tribulation had stricken such terror to the hearts of all, men and women alike, that brother forsook brother, uncle nephew and sister brother and oftentimes wife husband; nay (what is yet more extraordinary and well nigh incredible) fathers and mothers refused to visit or tend their very children. . . . Such was the multitude of those who died in the city by day and by night that it was an astonishment to hear tell thereof. . . . Many breathed their last in the open street, whilst other many, for all they died in their houses, made it known to the neighbours that they were dead rather by the stench of their rotting bodies than otherwise, and of these and others who died all about the whole city was full.

Italy had long been a melting pot of many different cultures. Invaders and trading partners from northern Europe, Africa, and Asia brought their unique styles of literature, art, and architecture to the bustling Italian port cities. Arab scholars shared their advanced systems of science, math, medicine, and philosophy. Late in the Middle Ages, soldiers returning from the Crusades—a series of wars fought by European Christians to capture the Holy Land (Palestine) from its Muslim rulers—brought a new appreciation of the learning and culture of the Middle East. Attracted by the spirit of learning and discovery, artists and scholars from many parts of the world came to Italy, adding their own talents to the rich cultural mix.

Location also led to wealth and changes in the social order. During most of the Middle Ages, there had been basically two social classes: the upper-class nobles and the lower-class laborers. As the city-states of Italy grew rich from trade, a new class emerged. This "middle class" included craftspeople who produced fine goods sold all over Europe, merchants who bought and sold goods for profit, and bankers who earned interest on the money they loaned to traders and nobles.

Some merchants and bankers grew enormously rich and powerful. By 1300, they dominated the politics and government of the largest city-states. The wealthy used their fortunes to build grand palaces and estates and to surround themselves with silks, furs, jewels, and other luxuries. To increase their own social standing and the glory of their city-states, many also became patrons of the arts and sciences. Their support of the work of painters, sculptors, architects, and scholars was the fuel that nourished the cultural achievements of the Renaissance.

Florence: Crossroads of Italy

"There is in my opinion," wrote one Renaissance traveler, "no region more sweet or pleasing in Italy or in any other part of Europe than that wherein Florence is placed." About fifty miles from the Mediterranean Sea, Florence sits in a fertile valley surrounded by rolling hills in the northern Italian region of Tuscany. The Arno River runs through the heart of the city, linking Florence with the Mediterranean. In Renaissance times, the Arno provided not only a trade route but also fresh drinking water, fish, sanitation, power for the city's mills, and plenty of water for Florence's main industry: cloth manufacturing. In the early 1300s, one-third of the

A merchant in bustling Florence bids his family good-bye before setting off on a journey to foreign markets. In this detail from a painting by fifteenth-century Italian Renaissance artist Filippino Lippi, the family is standing before one of the massive gateways in the walls of the city.

city's population of around one hundred thousand people earned a living washing, spinning, weaving, dyeing, and finishing wool. Many other Florentines worked transporting and trading cloth and other goods along the Arno and other trade routes. Major roads radiated from Florence in every direction, making the city a crossroads of travel and trade.

Banking grew up alongside trade. Florence was the financial

capital of Europe, with eighty banking houses lending money to merchants and governments all over the continent. In those times, there was no unified currency in Italy or Europe—each city-state and region produced its own money. By the time of the early Renaissance, the gold florin minted in Florence had become an international coin, accepted all over Europe and in many parts of the East.

The people of Florence prided themselves on their form of government. Unlike most of the other Italian city-states, Florence was a republic, in which many citizens participated in the shaping of laws and policies. The city's main governing body was the Signoria, run by nine elected

The Renaissance began in Florence, a thriving city-state in northern Italy. This fifteenth-century view shows the walls and watchtowers that enclosed the city on both sides of the Arno River.

officials from the city's leading families. The Signoria proposed laws, imposed taxes, and regulated activities such as road construction and trade. Under the Signoria was a complicated network of councils and committees, made up of thousands of officials who were responsible for approving or rejecting the laws and policies proposed by the Signoria and making sure all areas of government ran smoothly.

Only members of a trade guild could become government officials.

Money changes hands at a bank in Siena, a prosperous city-state just south of Florence. In this illustration from the cover of a tax register, angels add their blessings to the transactions.

Trade guilds were associations of businessmen and skilled workers that laid down rules ensuring that members maintained high standards in their line of work. There were twenty-one guilds. The wealthiest and most powerful Florentines—including lawyers, bankers, wool merchants, and cloth finishers—belonged to the seven greater guilds, called the *popolo grasso,* or "fat people." The fourteen lesser guilds, called the *popolo minuto,* or "little people," included simple tradesmen such as innkeepers, blacksmiths, tailors, stonemasons, and bakers. No more than four thousand men ever belonged to the guilds. The vast majority of Florentines—including all women as well as common wool workers and other day laborers—were excluded from membership and so had no say in the city's government.

Over time, Florence's limited democracy became even less democratic. Members of one wealthy family after another found ways to control the government, using "gifts" and favors to buy political appointments and influence votes. At the end of the 1300s, the leading power was the Albizzi family of wealthy wool merchants. The Albizzis dominated the government through a half century of turmoil and growth. During their rule, Florence fought off invading armies from the city-states of Milan and Naples and launched its own invasions against territories in Tuscany, conquering the Mediterranean port city of Pisa. These tumultuous times also saw some of the great achievements of the early Renaissance, including fine works of sculpture and architecture. But it was another family, more famous and even more powerful, that would lead Florence to its greatest glory: the Medici.

The ladies of the Albizzi family were noted for their elegance and gentility. This portrait of Giovanna Albizzi was painted in 1488 by the Italian master Domenico Ghirlandaio, shortly after the noble- woman's marriage into another prominent Florentine family.

Court of the Magi *by fifteenth-century Italian artist Benozzo Gozzoli depicts the biblical story of the three wise men from the East who journeyed to honor the infant Jesus—but with a Renaissance twist. That's young Lorenzo de' Medici wearing the crown, followed by his father, Piero, (on a white horse) and grandfather Cosimo (on the brown mule with gold-studded bridle).*

Medici Magnificence

In 1434, a power struggle between Florence's two wealthiest families ended when city leaders sent the head of the Albizzi family into exile and invited Cosimo de' Medici to run the government. The Medicis had made their fortune through banking. A shrewd politician, Cosimo used his family's vast wealth to buy the loyalty and support of government officials. Cosimo also poured large sums of money into scholarship and the arts. Fascinated by classical (ancient Greek and Roman) writings, he funded the work of scholars who searched for and translated lost manuscripts. His wealth also launched an ambitious building program. Florentines grumbled about the constant noise and dust as builders worked to

transform the city with magnificent new churches, monasteries, libraries, and family palaces. All were decorated with classical sculpture as well as fine new works of art, including statues and frescoes (wall paintings).

After Cosimo's death, his sickly son Piero briefly held the reins of power. Then, in 1469, Piero died and city leaders asked his twenty-one-year-old son Lorenzo to "take charge of the city and of the state." Lorenzo de' Medici had been well educated in business and politics. He was a brilliant scholar, a poet, and an energetic athlete who loved hunting and horseback riding. In 1478, when Pope Sixtus IV entered into a conspiracy with another powerful Florentine family to overthrow the Medicis, Lorenzo escaped by fighting off the assassins with his sword. The attack killed his younger brother, and Lorenzo resolved to tighten the Medicis' control of Florence. Rewriting the city's constitution, he created a new committee of seventy handpicked officials to control every aspect of the government, with himself as the group's absolute ruler. Although some Florentines objected, most saw Lorenzo as a wise and just ruler, and praised his efforts to ensure the city's peace and prosperity.

Lorenzo also continued the family tradition of support for scholarship and the arts. He filled his home with a wealth of antique art and ancient manuscripts, and surrounded himself with the brightest scholars, philosophers, poets, and artists of the day. Under his patronage, Florence blossomed as the cultural center of Europe and the heart of the Renaissance. For his brilliant intellectual and political leadership, Florentines honored him with the title Lorenzo the Magnificent.

A Golden Age Ends

In April 1492, lightning flashed from a clear sky and struck the cathedral of Florence. Taking this as a sign of coming disaster, Florentines were not surprised when, three days later, Lorenzo de' Medici died.

Lorenzo's son Piero was a weak and timid ruler. In 1494, when the armies of King Charles VIII of France marched through Italy, Piero surrendered several important territories without a fight. The outraged Florentines drove the Medicis from the city and turned to a new leader: the powerful monk Girolamo Savonarola.

In his fiery sermons, Savonarola threatened hellfire and damnation for all who refused to give up the luxuries of the new age and lead a pure, simple, God-fearing life. The terrified Florentines responded by building

LORENZO THE MAGNIFICENT

In 1508, Florentine politician and historian Francesco Guicciardini opened his *History of Florence* with a description of Lorenzo de' Medici. His portrait touches on both the positive and negative sides of Lorenzo's larger-than-life personality:

> Lorenzo possessed many outstanding qualities. He also had certain vices—some natural, others induced by necessity. He had such great authority that one may say that the city was not free in his time, even though it was rich in all those glories and good fortunes which a city may enjoy when free in name but in fact ruled as a tyrant by one of its citizens. . . . No one even of his enemies and critics denies that he had a brilliant and outstanding mind; and the proof is that for twenty-three years he ruled the city and constantly increased her power and glory, and he would be a fool who denied it. . . .
>
> He desired glory and success more than any man. One may criticize him for carrying this passion even into things of small importance, so that even in poetry, in games and other pursuits he would not permit any to imitate or compete with him, and was angry with those who did so. Even in greater things his ambition was excessive, for he wished to rival and compete with all the princes of Italy in everything. . . . Nevertheless, on the whole this ambition was praiseworthy and made him famous everywhere even outside Italy, for he strove to ensure that all the arts and talents should flourish more brilliantly in Florence than in any other city in Italy.

Lorenzo de' Medici's ambition, generosity, and lust for glory helped make Florence the political and cultural capital of the Italian Renaissance.

a giant bonfire—known as the "bonfire of the vanities"—in a public square. There they burned their cosmetics, hairpieces, jewelry, and playing cards, along with their classical and Renaissance books, works of art, and other "evil corrupters" of the human soul. A year later, tired of the monk's grim prophesies and strict reforms, the people turned against Savonarola and hanged and burned him in the same square. But by then, the great artists and scholars of the Renaissance had moved on. Florence's golden age was at an end.

Rome, Venice, and Beyond

As the glory of the Renaissance dwindled in Florence, Rome enjoyed a brief period as Europe's new cultural capital. The city was the center of the church in western Europe and ruler of the Papal States, a large group of territories in central Italy. But in the fourteenth century, conflicts had divided the church and weakened Rome. The court of the pope had been moved to France, and for a time two rival popes claimed power in Europe. Rome became a run-down country town where cows grazed among the crumbling ruins of ancient monuments.

Then, in the early 1400s, the church was reunited, and Pope Nicholas V began to rebuild Rome. Nicholas had a vision of a new city even more glorious than ancient Rome. Inviting artists, architects, and scholars from all over Italy, he began the work of building a fabulous Vatican—a separate city within Rome, set apart for the church. The popes who followed Nicholas made his dream a reality. Increasing Rome's control over the surrounding territories—sometimes waging war against the other Italian city-states—these ambitious leaders established the Papal States as one of Italy's great powers. They repaired the roads of Rome, rebuilt ancient bridges and walls, and adorned the Vatican with glorious churches, palaces, libraries, and gardens. In the early

In the turmoil following French attacks in 1494, the fanatical monk Savonarola became Florence's most powerful political leader. Denouncing greed and corruption in the church and in Florentine society, Savonarola called for strict reforms, including banning all nonreligious books and artwork.

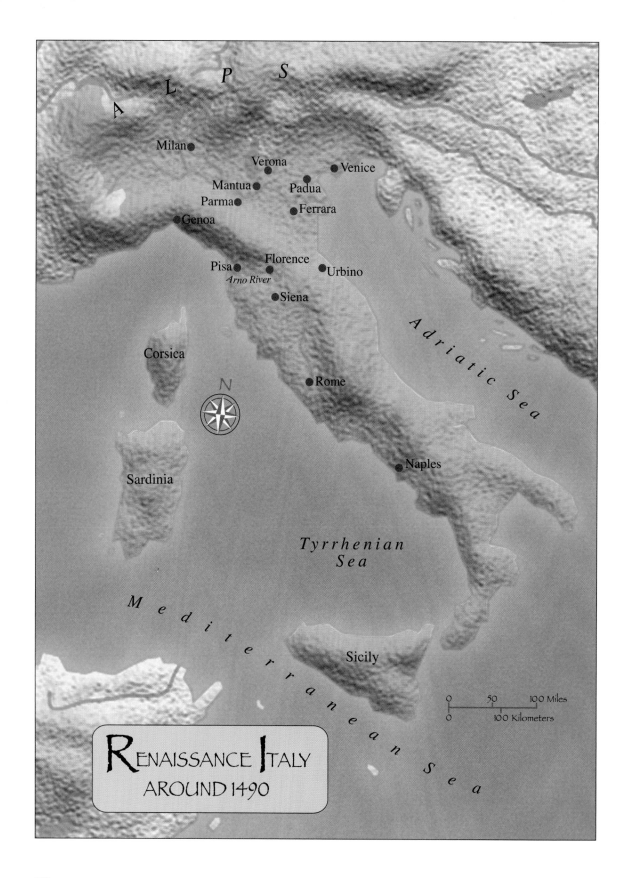

Renaissance Italy around 1490

1500s, under the patronage of Popes Julius II and Leo X (a son of Lorenzo de' Medici), artists including Leonardo da Vinci, Michelangelo, and Raphael created some of the most glorious works of Renaissance art.

In 1527, the armies of Holy Roman Emperor Charles V sacked, or captured and plundered, Rome. Mercenary soldiers destroyed buildings and artwork, imprisoned the pope, and killed some ten thousand Romans. The church lost much of its power for a time, and the artists and scholars fled.

Many of those who left Rome settled in Venice. This northern port city controlled an extensive Mediterranean trading empire. Wealthy Venetian merchants lavished money on the arts. Their enormous palaces overflowed with the creative output of artists and craftspeople: portraits and oil paintings, bronze statues, delicate glassware and mirrors, elaborate jewelry, books published by the city's many printers.

But even as beauty and culture reigned in Venice, the Italian Renaissance was beginning to fade. Throughout the sixteenth century, a series of battles among the city-states kept the peninsula in constant turmoil. Invasions by France, Spain, and the Holy Roman Empire brought suffering, death, and destruction, draining the energy and confidence of the Italian people. Although the invaders played a role in bringing about the end of the Italian Renaissance, they also helped carry its culture and learning to the rest of Europe. There the Renaissance spirit would survive and flourish.

CHAPTER TWO

A NEW AGE

"Now indeed," wrote one Florentine philosopher in the 1430s, "may every thoughtful spirit thank God that it has been permitted to him to be born in this new age." The people of the Renaissance knew they were living in remarkable times. A great explosion of learning and culture was transforming their world, bringing new ideas and achievements in many areas: art, architecture, literature, education, science, and philosophy.

Art and Architecture

Painting the World

The art of the Middle Ages focused mainly on religious themes, such as scenes from the Bible and portraits of Jesus and the saints. The style of paintings was often flat and stiff, as artists concentrated on creating symbolic representations of religious figures and events, rather than true-to-life images. Renaissance painters broke with the past, using new techniques to bring their art to life.

One of the most important painters of the early Renaissance was a Florentine named Giotto di Bondone. Sometimes called the Father of Western Painting, Giotto brought a new drama and realism to art. The people in his paintings had lifelike, expressive faces. His landscapes were so natural that the writer Boccaccio described them as "not so much similar to the originals, as real in themselves."

Later Renaissance painters perfected Giotto's style, which came to be known as naturalism. Carefully studying nature and the human body, they learned to create works of art that captured the movement and vitality of

the real world. Adding to the realism of their art was perspective—a technique for making paintings look three-dimensional. One of the first Renaissance painters to experiment with perspective was Masaccio. In the early 1400s, this young Florentine used perspective along with shadows and light to create art more lifelike than anything ever painted before.

Giotto, Masaccio, and other early Renaissance artists most often

In the early fourteenth century, the Florentine artist Giotto set a new course for Western painting. Turning away from the flat, rigid style of medieval art, he painted natural-looking people and realistic landscapes. In The Virgin's Suitors Praying before the Rods in the Temple, *Giotto depicts a Christian legend about the divine selection of Joseph as the husband of the Virgin Mary, mother of Christ.*

painted religious themes, just as medieval artists had. But naturalism gave their subjects a more down-to-earth manner, portraying even the saints in ordinary poses, with vivid human emotions. Over time, many artists began to paint nonreligious subjects, too: landscapes, portraits of wealthy patrons, the myths and gods of the ancient Greeks and Romans. Florentine painter Sandro Botticelli, a favorite of Lorenzo de' Medici, created many exquisite paintings on classical themes. One of the most famous paintings of the early Renaissance was Botticelli's *Birth of Venus*, which shows the Roman goddess of love and beauty rising from the sea.

The Birth of Venus *by Sandro Botticelli is one of the most famous paintings of the early Renaissance. The Roman goddess of love and beauty is shown being born out of the sea, just as Renaissance artists and scholars believed that they had been "reborn" through the glories of ancient Greece and Rome.*

This bronze relief panel from the east doors of Florence's Baptistery tells the biblical story of Joseph. Sculptor Lorenzo Ghiberti spent twenty-seven years completing the ten panels of the east doors, which are known today as the Gates of Paradise.

Bringing Sculpture to Life

Like Renaissance painters, sculptors also experimented with new ways to breathe life into their art. Early Renaissance sculpture often was in the form of reliefs—figures carved or molded to stand out from a flat surface. In 1401, the wool merchants' guild of Florence commissioned, or hired, sculptor Lorenzo Ghiberti to make a set of bronze panels for the north doors of the Baptistery, a church building used for baptisms. Ghiberti spent twenty years designing, casting, and finishing the doors, then another twenty-seven years making a second set for the Baptistery's east doors. Each of the panels in Ghiberti's doors shows a different scene from the Bible. The tiny figures are graceful and lifelike, and the relief background uses perspective to create a sense of space and depth. The famous sculptor Michelangelo praised Ghiberti's doors as "worthy of the gates of paradise."

Ghiberti's work was inspired by classical art. The ancient Greeks and Romans had created masterpieces of sculpture celebrating the beauty and power of their gods, and scholars digging among the ruins of Rome had recovered many of these lost treasures. Early Renaissance sculptors studied the classical style, imitating it in their reliefs as well as in statues of the Roman gods, Christian saints, biblical heroes, and wealthy patrons posed heroically on horseback.

The Florentine sculptor Donatello was just seventeen when he visited Rome. Returning home, he combined the classical style with his own personal vision, creating statues famous for their power and realism. Donatello's bronze *David,* commissioned by Cosimo de' Medici in 1430, was the first nude statue since ancient times. Like classical art, it celebrated the beauty of the human body, yet it also seemed to express the youthful, vibrant Renaissance spirit. One sixteenth-century art historian declared that the statue was "so natural . . . that it is almost impossible . . . to believe that it was not molded on the living form."

A Revolution in Architecture

When Ghiberti began designing the Baptistery doors in 1401, Florentine sculptor Filippo Brunelleschi—angry at being passed over for the commission—declared that he would give up sculpture and become an architect instead. Traveling to Rome with his young friend Donatello, Brunelleschi spent several years studying the ruins. He sketched ancient Roman temples, climbed on crumbling rooftops to peek beneath the tiles, and pondered classical texts on architecture. Gradually he unlocked the secrets of the ancients, including the use of perspective and the mathematical rules behind the perfect proportions of the different parts of the buildings.

Back in Florence, Brunelleschi went to work on a challenging project: the dome of the city cathedral. Construction of the cathedral of Florence had begun in 1296, but by the early 1400s, the towering monument still was not finished. The building was so huge that no one knew how to build the grand dome that was supposed to top it. Using his new knowledge, Brunelleschi solved the problem. His soaring and graceful dome—built as two domes, one inside the other, for support and strength—was completed in 1436. The largest dome on the largest church in the world, it was a fitting monument to the greatness of Renaissance Florence.

As Brunelleschi's fame spread, his ideas had a dramatic effect on Renaissance art. Florentine scholar Leon Battista Alberti explained the architect's mathematical rules for perspective and proportion in the book *On Painting,* written in 1435, and painters and sculptors applied those techniques to their works. Architects copied Brunelleschi's building style. Medieval architecture had often been angular and dramatic, with soaring

The construction of Filippo Brunelleschi's enormous dome for the cathedral of Florence marked the beginning of Italian Renaissance architecture. Today the strong but graceful dome still towers over the city.

ceilings, pointed arches, and surfaces crowded with decorations. Now new churches, hospitals, libraries, and grand homes sprang up all over Florence, built in what is known today as the Renaissance style—simple, elegant, and beautifully proportioned, with slender columns and curving arches. The city-state became famous as the site of some of the most beautiful and original architecture in Europe. "Whoever wants to build in Italy today," one Italian writer boasted in the 1490s, "must turn to Florence for architects."

The High Renaissance

The discoveries and experimentation of the fourteenth and fifteenth centuries reached their peak in the High Renaissance. This brief period, from around 1495 to 1527, saw some of the most notable creative achievements in the history of art. Even as Italy was plagued by invading armies and internal strife, three great artists gave the world their finest work: Leonardo, Michelangelo, and Raphael.

Born in 1452, Leonardo da Vinci lived and worked in Florence, Milan, Rome, and France. A genius with an incredible variety of interests, Leonardo excelled as painter, sculptor, architect,

Mona Lisa *represented Leonardo da Vinci's vision of ideal beauty. The artist used light and shadow, along with blurred outlines on the mouth and eyes, to give his portrait a haunting sense of mystery that still fascinates viewers today.*

writer, musician, inventor, engineer, mathematician, and scientist. His two most famous masterpieces, *The Last Supper* and *Mona Lisa,* demonstrate his dedication to painting not just the physical person but "what is going on in the mind."

Leonardo kept notebooks filled with his observations, sketches, and ideas. He made drawings of the inner body—the

LEONARDO DA VINCI: UNIVERSAL MASTER

Leonardo da Vinci's restless curiosity marked an important change in the direction of the Italian Renaissance. Before Leonardo, Renaissance scholars, artists, and architects had been content to study and imitate the classical masters. But Leonardo believed in seeking his own truths by observing the world around him. Following his example, the artists and scholars of the High Renaissance experimented, explored, and achieved new brilliance and originality in their work.

In this passage from one of his notebooks, Leonardo explains the importance of observation to the artist:

The mind of the painter must resemble a mirror, which always takes the colour of the object it reflects and is completely occupied by the images of as many objects as are in front of it. Therefore you must know, Oh Painter! that you cannot be a good one if you are not the universal master of representing by your art every kind of form produced by nature. And this you will not know how to do if you do not see them, and retain them in your mind. Hence as you go through the fields, turn your attention to various objects, and, in turn look now at this thing and now at that, collecting a store of divers[e] facts selected and chosen from those of less value.

heart, lungs, and muscles; a child in its mother's womb—that were beautiful and sometimes remarkably accurate. Most amazing of all were his sketches and plans for later inventions including the alarm clock, life jacket, cannon, armored tank, submarine, and a flying machine.

Like Leonardo, Michelangelo Buonarroti was a man of many interests and abilities: sculptor, painter, architect, poet, engineer. As a boy, Michelangelo attended a school for sculptors that had been set up by Lorenzo de' Medici. Lorenzo was so impressed with the young artist's talents that he invited Michelangelo to live in the Medici household. There the boy developed his artistic talents, crafting skillful copies of the

God reaches to give the divine spark of life to Adam, in this well-known scene from Michelangelo's huge fresco on the ceiling of the Sistine Chapel. The temperamental artist often fought with his patron, Pope Julius II, during the four years it took to complete the paintings. Finally, in 1512, when the pope complained the project was taking too long, Michelangelo stormed off, declaring his work done.

classical statues in the Medici gardens.

After Lorenzo's death in 1492, Michelangelo divided his time between Florence and Rome. His masterpieces in marble—especially the *Pietà* (a sculpture of Mary holding the body of her son Jesus) and the fourteen-foot-tall *David*—made him famous throughout Italy. In his sculptures, Michelangelo strove not just to imitate nature but to express the divine beauty in all God's creations. He believed that his life's work was to reveal the noble art hidden within the natural world. When someone once asked if it was hard to carve the *David,* the sculptor replied, "The difficult thing was finding the block of marble in which David was. After that it was merely a matter of removing everything that was not David."

Michelangelo's most famous paintings cover the ceiling of the Sistine Chapel in Rome. In four years of backbreaking labor, he painted more than three hundred figures that tell stories from the biblical book of Genesis, from the creation of the world to Noah. Each scene is a breathtaking work of art, and their combined beauty, power, and emotion have carried Michelangelo's fame through the centuries.

In his time, Michelangelo was almost as famous for his fiery temper as his art. In contrast, the third genius of the High Renaissance, Raphael Santi, was known for his sweet and gentle nature. Raphael's personality carried over into his art. His many paintings of the Madonna (Mary, the mother of Christ) glow with a soft, graceful beauty. Raphael's most ambitious project was the painting of frescoes in Pope Julius II's apartments in the Vatican Palace in Rome. While Michelangelo worked nearby in the Sistine Chapel, Raphael decorated the pope's walls and ceilings with a series of paintings representing ideals such as wisdom, knowledge, and virtue. Most celebrated is the *School of Athens*. In this grand fresco, the Greek philosophers Plato and Aristotle stroll among the scholars and scientists of the Renaissance world.

Holy Family with a Palm Tree *by Raphael shows Joseph and Mary with the baby Jesus. Raphael's paintings are famous for their balance, naturalism, and gentle beauty.*

A New Language for a New Age

In 1302, nobleman Dante Alighieri was banished from Florence when his political party fell from power. Wandering across Italy, Dante composed a long poem called *The Divine Comedy*. The poem tells the story of Dante's imaginary journey through hell, purgatory, and heaven, with the ancient Roman poet Virgil as his guide along the way. Today *The Divine Comedy* is known both as one of the finest examples of medieval writing and as the spark that gave rise to a new kind of literature.

During the Middle Ages, educated people throughout Europe wrote mainly in Latin, the language of the ancient Romans and of the Catholic Church. Each region of Italy spoke its own form of Italian, but this vernacular, or native speech, was considered too vulgar for serious writing. Dante wanted a wide audience for his poetry. He wrote *The Divine Comedy* in the vernacular of Florence, adding elements from Latin and other languages to create a new Italian language, elegant enough for fine writing but also useful in everyday speech. Dante's creation became the language of the Italian Renaissance.

Several years after *The Divine Comedy,* Francesco Petrarca, known in English as Petrarch, wrote a series of love poems in the new Italian. Like Dante, Petrarch spent much of his life wandering across Italy. Somewhere in his travels, he met a married woman named Laura, who

Dante was an avid student of philosophy and poetry. His Divine Comedy *made the vernacular of Florence the literary language of the Italian Renaissance.*

became the unattainable love of his life. Each of Petrarch's 366 poems to Laura is a sonnet, a form of poetry with fourteen lines. Because of the perfection of his sonnets, which bring Laura to life and convey the lover's longing in beautiful, flowing Italian, Petrarch is often called the first modern poet. Here is a portion of one of Petrarch's love sonnets:

> *My sweet thoughts sometime do pleasure bring;*
> *But by and by, the cause of my disease*
> *Gives me a pang that inwardly doth sting,*
> *When that I think what grief it is again*
> *To live and lack the thing should rid my pain.*

Petrarch also wrote poetry, essays, and letters in Latin. A great admirer of the elegant style and rhythms of the ancient Roman writers, he passed along his love of classical literature to his friend and student Giovanni Boccaccio of Florence. Like Petrarch, Boccaccio wrote in Latin, composing poetry and books on science and mythology. But he is most famous for his writings in Italian, including the first major European collection of short stories in the vernacular, the *Decameron* (see page 9).

Other Italian Renaissance writers were inspired by the style and themes of the ancient Roman playwrights. Most early Renaissance plays were written in Latin and performed solely for the wealthy in their grand estates and palaces. In the sixteenth century, Italian playwrights began writing in the vernacular, and in 1565 the first permanent theater in Italy was built near Venice. Soon the best artists and architects of the day were designing stage sets for public and private theaters throughout Italy. The architect Brunelleschi, who worked on "special effects" for plays performed during religious festivals in Florence, once created a giant sphere filled with sparkling lights, which opened to let the angel Gabriel float down to earth.

The Printing Press

In the early Renaissance, a writer who wanted to study classical texts had to visit a private library founded by a church or university, where the manuscripts were so valuable they were sometimes chained to the tables. Books were priceless because they were rare. Manuscripts had to be painstakingly copied out by hand, usually by monks or professional scribes, or printed from hand-carved wooden blocks. A single manuscript might take a year or more to reproduce and cost as much as a skilled craftsperson earned in a month.

In the 1450s, German inventor Johannes Gutenberg began turning out books on his new printing press. The printing press used movable metal letters that could be arranged in any order to form the text on a page. Suddenly it was possible to print hundreds of copies of a manuscript quickly and inexpensively.

By the year 1500, printing presses were operating all over Italy, with more than one hundred in Venice alone. The first printed books were mainly religious works and copies of ancient Greek and Roman manuscripts. Soon practical books and pamphlets on mathematics, medicine, and housekeeping appeared, along with poetry and prose in the vernacular by Renaissance scholars and writers such as Alberti, Petrarch, and Boccaccio. These new writings reached not only the well educated and wealthy but also ordinary merchants, bankers, artists, and skilled workers.

The widespread availability of printed books helped encourage the growth of literacy—the ability to read and write. Literacy was already on the rise among the middle class. For businessmen and skilled workers, knowing how to read contracts and write orders and reports were important business tools. By the late fifteenth century, many professional organizations such as the trade guilds of Florence required that members be able to read and write. However, few unskilled laborers or farmers could read.

As literacy grew, so did the need for schools. The children of the wealthy were often educated at home by private tutors. Middle-class parents might send their children to a religious school at a monastery or convent, or to one of the new private elementary schools set up by scholars in the larger city-states. More boys than girls went to school, and usually only boys got to continue their education at a university. Again, few day laborers or country folk could afford the time or the fees required for schooling.

Advances in Science

In Renaissance times, there were no scientists as we know them today. The Latin word *scientia* simply means "knowledge," and Renaissance scientists might seek knowledge in philosophy, art, anatomy (the structure of the body), medicine, mathematics, and many other studies.

IF YOU LIVED IN RENAISSANCE FLORENCE

If you had been born in Florence during the Italian Renaissance, your way of life would have been determined by the facts of your birth—whether you were a girl or a boy; wealthy or poor; merchant, banker, skilled craftsperson, or day laborer. With this chart you can trace the course your life might have taken as a middle-class citizen of Renaissance Florence.

You were born in Florence. . . .

As a Boy . . .   As a Girl . . .

You live in a tall stone house on a crowded city street, above your father's workshop. Your parents are warm and affectionate, but your father is often away from home. You enjoy singing and dancing, playing with marbles or dolls, and playing tag and other games with your brothers and sisters.

At age 6 or 7, you begin school. For 4 to 6 hours each day, you study reading, writing, math, and Latin, and perhaps other subjects such as logic (reasoning), rhetoric (speaking and writing skills), and poetry.

At age 10 or 11, if you plan to learn a trade, your father may pay a master craftsman to take you in and train you. You live in the master's household, train in his shop, and may be educated alongside his children.

Around age 15, you may begin attending a university, where your studies include music, advanced math and Latin, astronomy, and perhaps history, geography, philosophy, or law. If you are an apprentice, you can remain at your master's shop as an employee or try to join a guild and open your own shop.

As an adult, you spend most of your time at work or talking business and politics in the squares and taverns. You serve on a government committee and continue your education by reading, studying, and debating philosophy and science with the scholars. You marry around age 35 and are the undisputed master of your household.

At age 6 or 7, you begin school. You learn to read and write, and to do enough basic math to run a household. After a few years, you leave school and finish your education at home, where your mother teaches you to cook, spin, sew, and play the lute or another musical instrument.

At age 15 or 16, you marry the man your father chooses, usually someone about twice your age. Your father gives you a dowry of cash, clothes, and other possessions to bring with you to your husband's home.

As a wife and mother you spend nearly all your time at home, raising your children and running the household, which includes one or two servants. Your husband is the head of the household, and you are expected to love, honor, and obey him.

If your husband dies before you, his family may allow you to remain in his home as long as your children are young, or you may be sent to live with your father or another male relative, who takes control of your property. You may be allowed to continue to operate your husband's business, but only for a short time, until you remarry.

In your old age, you are respected for your wisdom and experience. When you die, you are wrapped in a white sheet called a burial shroud and laid in a stone tomb inside a church or a special building set aside for burials. Women can make wills leaving their dowry to their children or other relatives, and both men and women may leave money to a church, monastery, or convent, so that the priests, monks, or nuns will pray for their souls.

Religion and tradition shaped their beliefs, and they relied mainly on written texts on science and philosophy instead of observation and experimentation, the tools of modern science. Many scientists turned to magic, astrology (predicting human affairs by the position of the stars and planets), and numerology (the study of magical numbers) to explain the natural world. In the *Decameron*, Boccaccio reflected the common belief that the Black Death was caused by "the influence of the heavenly bodies or . . . God's just anger with our wicked deeds."

Over time, scientists began to question the authority of the ancient texts and to seek their own answers. Renaissance artists were the first to use the evidence of their eyes to unlock the mysteries of the natural world. Painters and sculptors studied the world around them so that they could portray it more realistically. Leonardo da Vinci dissected more than thirty corpses to understand the human body and made hundreds of drawings of human anatomy. Insisting that the only way to understand something is through observation and experimentation, he filled his notebooks with ideas and discoveries on plant and animal life, mathematics, mechanics, chemistry, light and vision, sound, the nature of water, and a

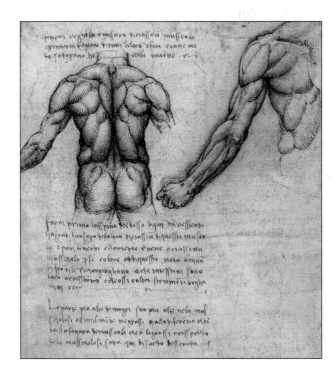

Leonardo da Vinci's remarkably detailed, often beautiful sketches of plants, animals, and human anatomy blurred the line between science and art.

wealth of other subjects. "Experience," he declared, "teaches how . . . nature acts among mortals."

Adopting the same "seeing is believing" attitude, Renaissance doctors began moving toward more modern medicine. Since medieval times, medical students had been educated mainly from manuscripts written by the ancient Roman physician Galen. Unfortunately, Galen's conclusions on human anatomy were based on dissections of monkeys, pigs, and dogs. In 1543, Andreas Vesalius, a scholar from Flanders teaching at the University of Padua in northeast Italy, published his own anatomy text, based on dissections of human corpses. Vesalius believed that medical students should be educated by reading his book and witnessing human dissections. At first, doctors were horrified by his methods, but in time his work led to a greater understanding of the human body and better treatment of illness and injuries.

Perhaps the most dramatic advances in science took place in astronomy, the study of the planets and other heavenly bodies. At the dawn of the Renaissance, most people accepted the explanation of the heavens adopted by the Catholic Church—that God had created the earth as the center of the universe and set the sun and stars in orbit around it. In 1543, the church banned a book by Polish astronomer Nicolaus Copernicus, which concluded that the earth and the other planets actually revolved around the sun.

In the twilight of the Italian Renaissance, Galileo Galilei pursued his own studies of the solar system. Born in Pisa, Galileo was an astronomer and mathematician who often got into trouble for challenging traditional scientific beliefs. Building the first telescope powerful enough to observe the night sky, he discovered four of the moons that orbit Jupiter as well as the billions of stars that make up the Milky Way. His book *Dialogue Concerning the Two Chief World Systems,* published in 1632, supported Copernicus's theory that the earth revolves around the sun. Church leaders were outraged. Charging Galileo with heresy—the expression of opinions contrary to the teachings of the church—a crime punishable by death, they forced him to take back his findings. But the truth was too powerful to be silenced. Over the next century, the power of the church would fade and Galileo's discoveries, along with his methods of observation and experimentation, would be embraced by scientists all across Europe.

CHAPTER THREE

THE
POWER OF
THE CHURCH

At the beginning of the Renaissance, practically all of Italy was Christian and nearly all Christians were Catholic. Religion was more than a set of beliefs and traditions. To the people of the Italian Renaissance, it was a way of life, shaping their society and influencing their attitudes, interests, and actions from the cradle to the grave.

Faith in Everyday Life

The center of Christianity is Jesus Christ, whose history is told in the New Testament of the Bible. Christians believe that Christ was the Son of God. He was born as a man to redeem humankind from sin and provide hope for eternal life in heaven, through his own life, death, and resurrection (rising from the dead). Christ taught his followers to lead a moral life, to love God, and to "love your neighbor as yourself" (Matthew 22:39).

The Catholic Church celebrates God's grace (the gift of the redeeming of sins) through rituals called sacraments, believed to have begun with Christ. In the thirteenth century, the church gave its stamp of approval to seven sacraments. These ceremonies marked some of the most important events in the life of nearly every man, woman, and child in Renaissance Italy:

Baptism: Every newborn was initiated into the church through baptism. During this sacrament, a priest anointed (touched or rubbed) the infant with holy water, washing away its sins and purifying its soul. Afterward, the family returned home to celebrate the happy occasion with a feast of sweets and other delicacies.

Confirmation: Children who had reached the "age of reason," usually around age six or seven, were confirmed, or accepted as full members of

Pope Leo X (center) *was a generous patron of the arts who supported hundreds of poets and commissioned magnificent tapestries and paintings, including this portrait by Raphael. To pay for it all, Leo engaged in some very unpopelike practices. He once arrested a number of cardinals on phony charges, hanged one of them, and then offered the rest their freedom in exchange for hefty "fines."*

39

the church. Dressed in their finest clothes, they stood before a bishop, who anointed them with oil and blessed them through the laying on of hands.

Communion: The child who had been confirmed was eligible to join his or her parents in Holy Communion, a sacrament that recalls the Last Supper—Christ's final meal with his followers before his crucifixion (death on the cross). During Communion, worshippers eat bread and sip wine, which are believed to change into the Body and Blood of Christ.

Confession: Before receiving Communion, worshippers were required to confess their sins to a priest, who assigned a penance—usually a certain number of prayers or good deeds—before granting forgiveness. Confession was sometimes made out loud during the church service, with all worshippers reciting a general confession of sins. Toward the end of the Renaissance, the practice of private confession became more common, allowing worshippers to whisper their sins to the priest alone.

Extreme unction: A person who was dying sent for a priest to hear his or her last confession and grant forgiveness of sins. Without this essential sacrament, the soul of the believer could have a difficult time entering heaven.

Holy orders: Men who became priests received the sacrament of holy orders, granting them the grace and spiritual power to dedicate their lives to Christ. (Men becoming monks and women becoming nuns took vows— promises made to God, which weren't considered sacraments but were just as solemn and binding.)

Marriage: A Renaissance wedding was both a serious and joyous occasion, signifying the continuation and renewal of the family line. According to church teachings, the bond created by the sacrament of marriage could never be broken; there was no such thing as divorce in Renaissance Italy. However, the church could sometimes be persuaded to grant an annulment, examining the marriage and declaring that, for one reason or another, it had never been valid.

A Florentine couple celebrate their marriage. In Renaissance Italy, marriage was a very practical affair, with matches often arranged by parents to strengthen a family's financial or social position.

Celebrating the Faith

Most sacraments were celebrated in the local church, the center of life in Renaissance Italy. In large cities and small towns, the sound of the church bells marked the hours of the day. Many people went to church almost every day, attending either early morning mass or the evening worship service known as vespers. The entire family might go to morning mass — a service conducted by a priest, who led the faithful in prayer, served Communion, and delivered a sermon on the Bible and proper Christian behavior. Attending morning mass with the family was often the only outing of the day for a middle-class or an upper-class married woman.

Religious festivals provided another chance to get out in the world and have some fun while celebrating the faith. Festivals were public holidays marking important dates in the church calendar. Most numerous were the feast days honoring saints. Every Italian city-state had its own patron saint — the spirit of a holy person believed to be the city's special protector. The patroness of Siena, in central Italy, was the first and most beloved of all saints: Mary, the mother of Christ. Siena celebrated one of the principal feast days of Saint Mary with music, parades, and wild bareback horse races through the city streets.

The patron saint of Florence was Saint John the Baptist. The festival of Saint John called for several days of joyous tribute, both to the saint and to the glory of the city itself. Houses and shops were hung with silk and gold tapestries, and colorful processions wound through the streets: jugglers and stilt walkers, horsemen bearing tall banners representing the different trades, worshippers dressed as saints and angels, priests carrying sacred relics (articles believed to be the physical remains of saints, or items that once belonged to them). There were feasts, games, bonfires, horse races, mock battles, and plays. "The whole city," reported a Florentine during one of the festivals, "is given over to revelry and feasting, with so many fifes and music, songs, dances, and other festivities and merrymaking, that this earth seems like a paradise."

In between solemn church services and lively festivals, people showed their religious devotion in many other ways: in private prayer and Bible study; in the religious paintings and crosses that adorned their homes; in charitable giving to religious foundations, hospitals, orphanages, and the needy. Trade guilds often required members to give clothing

The Miracle of the Relic of the Holy Cross *by Venetian painter Giovanni Mansueti tells the story of a miracle performed by a bit of wood from the cross on which Jesus was crucified. According to the story, the golden cross containing the sacred wood was carried at the funeral of a wealthy man who had not believed in its power. When the funeral procession reached the church, the cross suddenly became too heavy to carry over the threshold.*

or other gifts to the poor once a year. The wealthiest guilds and individuals poured money into the construction and upkeep of churches and other religious sites.

In the larger city-states, charitable organizations were formed to put religion into practice. Florence had a number of these organizations, or

Florentines considered it a religious duty to give to those less fortunate. These charity-minded citizens are offering comfort to hospital patients.

fraternities, each with its own mission: feeding the poor, tending the sick, caring for orphans and abandoned children, distributing prayers and hymns printed in the vernacular. One fraternity, known as the Compagnia dei Neri, or Company of Blacks, for the color of the hooded gowns worn by its members, cared for prisoners who had been sentenced to death. The Neri offered food, comfort, and religious ministry to the condemned, escorted them to their execution, and buried their bodies afterward.

Education and Art

Just as faith was a powerful force in everyday life during the Italian Renaissance, so was the institution of the church itself. Since the Middle Ages, the Catholic Church had played a major role in shaping people's thoughts and ideas not only in religion but in all areas of life, largely through its control of education. For centuries, the only schools in Italy were church schools, where young men destined for the priesthood or life in a monastery were educated. That meant that very few people outside the clergy could read or write. Those who were literate often found their choice of reading materials controlled by the church. Before the invention of the printing press, most books were hand-copied in monasteries, where monks labored over beautifully decorated manuscripts of the Bible and other texts.

A NUN'S COMPLAINT

The world of the Italian Renaissance was dominated by men. They had the political power, education, and wealth, and they played the leading role in art, literature, and science. A few extraordinary women managed to gain behind-the-scenes political power or to become noted writers, artists, or art patrons. But most Renaissance women lived quiet, dependent lives, under the thumb of fathers or husbands who considered them weak, imperfect, and in need of firm guidance and control.

Some young women in Renaissance Italy embraced the religious life, taking nuns' vows and living in convents, where they could study, teach, and serve God. Thousands of others, such as Arcangela Tarabotti of Venice, were sent to convents because their fathers could not or would not provide a sufficient dowry for them to marry. Tarabotti wrote this fierce attack on fathers who forced their daughters to commit themselves to a lifetime of unwilling solitude and service:

> It is well known that the majority of nuns cannot attain perfection because they are forced to the religious life by the force exerted by their fathers and kin. . . . It seems to me, when I see one of these unfortunate girls so betrayed by their own fathers, that I see that which happens to the little song bird, which in its pure simplicity, there between the leaves of the trees or along the banks of rivers, goes with sweet murmur and with gentle harmony stroking the ear and consoling the heart of he who hears it, when there comes a sly net and it is caught and deprived of its dear liberty. In the same way these unhappy girls, born under an unfortunate star, pass the years of their innocent girlhood, and with a tongue tinged with milk singing pretty lovesongs, and with their tender limbs forming graceful movements, please the ear and delight the soul of the base fathers who, deceitful, weaving nets of deception, think of nothing but to remove them from sight as soon as possible and so bury them alive in cloisters [convents] for the whole of their lives, bound with indissoluble [permanent] knots.

By the thirteenth century, the growing middle class had recognized the value of literacy. Parents began sending their children to school to prepare for careers in business or trade. Many students went to religious schools in monasteries and convents. There, along with reading, writing, and math, teachers emphasized church teachings. Central to every lesson was the belief that the Bible was the source of all knowledge and that the purpose of study was to glorify God and prepare the soul for eternity. The young person who asked thoughtful questions about science, philosophy, or the nature of humankind and the world earned a thrashing with the master's whip or cane.

The proper purpose of art, too, was to glorify God. During the Middle Ages and early Renaissance, nearly all art was concerned with religious themes, and the church was the most important art patron. Artists and architects were commissioned to build spectacular churches and chapels and to decorate them with religious paintings and sculptures.

In the High Renaissance, religion continued to inspire art, as the church commissioned major works such as Michelangelo's paintings on the ceiling of the Sistine Chapel. Religion also remained an important element in books and education. But new ideas were changing the way people thought about themselves and the world, loosening the church's hold on learning, art, science, and everyday life. In time, the new thinking of the Renaissance would lead some to challenge the church itself.

Corruption and Reform

When Giovanni de' Medici went to Rome to become a cardinal in 1492, his father, Lorenzo, warned him that the Holy City was a "sink of all iniquities [wickedness]," where "at present one sees such a lack of virtue." Wickedness had grown up alongside wealth and power. The church not only ruled the Papal States, it was also the largest landowner in Italy—in fact, in all of western Europe. Popes generally were chosen not for their superior faith and virtue but for their political skills and family connections. They frequently meddled in politics to increase their power, siding with one leader or political party against another—as had happened in 1478, when Pope Sixtus IV joined in the assassination plot against Lorenzo de' Medici. Popes also cemented their power by appointing friends and relatives to high-ranking positions in the church, a practice

Catholic cardinals in rich vestments file past a watchful crowd of Roman citizens. Many of the people of Renaissance Europe were concerned that, behind all its pomp and ceremony, the church was growing increasingly greedy and corrupt.

that came to be known as nepotism, from the Italian word for "nephew." Sixtus made five of his nephews cardinals and even appointed a favorite servant bishop of Parma.

Many church officials lived in luxury and self-indulgence. Italians joked about the "humble" parish priests who got fat from raiding the church treasury and drunk from sampling the Communion wine, who stumbled over their Latin during church

47

THE FATHER OF PROTESTANTISM

The Renaissance popes had a vision of a united Christian empire, with Rome as its glorious heart. With this end in mind, they built the power of the church and commissioned Italy's greatest artists and architects to beautify the Holy City. But their dreams vanished in war and reform—especially the Reformation launched by Martin Luther. In the Reformation, a new form of Christianity, Protestantism, broke away from the Catholic Church. Today Protestantism includes many denominations, or branches, including the Baptist, Episcopal, Lutheran, Methodist, and Presbyterian churches.

In this essay written in 1520, Luther rejects the authority of the clergy to intercede between believers and God, maintaining that salvation comes from faith alone:

> It does not help the soul if the body puts on sacred vestments as the priests and clergy do. It does not help even when the body is in church or in holy places, or when busy with sacred affairs; nor when the body is offering prayers, keeping fasts, or making pilgrimages, and doing other good works, which are performed only in and through the body. It must surely be something quite different which brings religion and freedom to the soul. For even a sinful man, or a hypocrite and pretender, may have all the afore-named things, do these works, and follow these ways. Also, this is the way to make men nothing but sheer hypocrites. Further it does no harm to the soul if the body wears worldly clothes, tarries in worldly places, eats, drinks, does not go on pilgrimages, nor keep the appointed hours of prayer; and if it neglects all the works that hypocrites perform, as already said.
>
> The only means, whether in heaven or on earth, whereby the soul can live, and be religious, free, and Christian, is the holy Gospel, the word of God preached by Christ. . . . Christ came for no other object than to preach the word of God. Moreover all apostles, bishops, priests, and the whole clergy, were called and instituted only for the sake of the word; although, unfortunately, things happen differently nowadays.

services and broke their vows of purity in secret visits to the nuns in their convents. Italian writer Masuccio Salernitano described traveling monks who made a living through trickery: "They cheat, steal . . . , and when they are at the end of their resources, they set up as saints and work miracles. . . . [They] bring with them confederates who pretend to be blind or afflicted with some mortal disease, and often touching the hem of the monk's cowl, or the relics which he carries, are healed before the eyes of the multitude."

By the early 1500s, people throughout Europe were grumbling about the corruption within the church and calling for reform. Many criticized Pope Leo X (the former Giovanni de' Medici), who went on a frenzy of fund-raising to finance the rebuilding of Saint Peter's Church in Rome. Leo raised a fortune by creating thirty-one new cardinals, who each paid a large fee for the privilege. The pope also joined forces with a German banking house to sell indulgences—papers that ensured the buyer forgiveness for all sins, past, present, and future. For just a few coins, "indulgence preachers" promised, sinners could escape hell's fire and buy their way into heaven.

One person who was especially outraged by the sale of indulgences and other corrupt church practices was a German monk named Martin Luther. Luther maintained that only faith in Christ could save the believer—not indulgences, prayers, good deeds, or blessings granted on God's behalf by a priest. In 1517, he nailed his Ninety-five Theses (a list of criticisms of the church) to the door of a church in Wittenberg, Germany. Pope Leo declared the German monk a heretic and banished him from the church. But Luther's ideas swiftly gained support throughout Europe, launching the Protestant Reformation. This religious revolution shook the foundations of the Catholic Church and gave rise to a new branch of Christianity.

CHAPTER FOUR

The Impact of Humanism

The Renaissance explosion of art and learning would never have happened without a new way of thinking called humanism. The humanists turned away from the medieval world's focus on saving souls and preparing for eternity. Their new philosophy did not deny God. But it did emphasize the importance of human affairs, encouraging human beings to question, explore, and achieve their full God-given potential.

The New Learning

The father of humanism was Petrarch, the fourteenth-century poet and scholar whose love sonnet appears on page 33. Petrarch was fascinated by classical literature. He devoted himself to the study of forgotten Latin manuscripts and imitated their elegant language and style in his own writings. Disgusted with the warfare and strife of his times, Petrarch turned to what he saw as the wisdom of the ancients. Outlining a "moral philosophy" that centered on the importance of the individual, he urged a return to the ancient Roman educational system, which was designed to give citizens the knowledge and virtue needed for a life of useful service. In 1341, in recognition of Petrarch's contributions to literature and society, the people of Rome revived an ancient custom, crowning him poet laureate—number-one poet of Italy.

The scholars of fourteenth-century Italy were electrified by Petrarch's philosophy, which they called the "new learning." Many began to see themselves as "new Romans"—descendants of the remarkable ancient Greek and Roman civilizations, who were destined to lead Italy to a new golden age of culture and glory. Eager to learn all they could about the ancient world, these early humanists went on a giant scavenger hunt. Fanning out all over Europe, they searched the dusty shelves of monastery libraries, hunting down Greek and Latin manuscripts. Valuable letters, speeches, books, and plays were discovered in stacks of

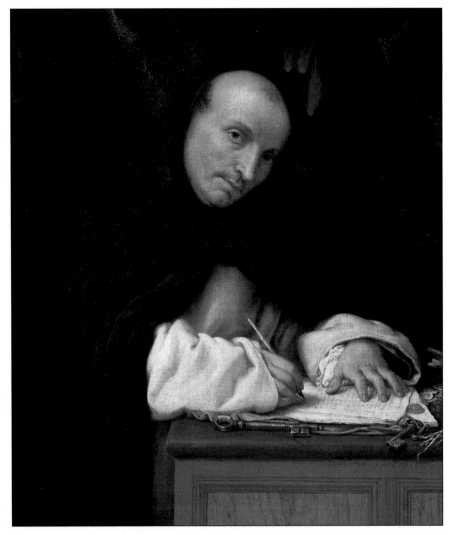

A monk from the Dominican order copies out a document. For centuries, monasteries were a center of literacy, and the ancient texts preserved in their libraries helped fuel the "new learning" of the Renaissance.

wastepaper. One scholar found a rare Latin manuscript, "covered in dust and mould," in a dingy storage room that he described as "dark and gloomy . . . , of a type in which not even those condemned to death would be incarcerated."

Some humanists seeking original Greek texts journeyed as far as Constantinople (modern-day Istanbul), the Greek-speaking capital of

PETRARCH'S LETTER TO FUTURE GENERATIONS

The father of humanism introduced a modern view of humankind that emphasized the importance of individuals and their work. In his *Letter to Posterity*, Petrarch led the way to a greater self-awareness by examining his own life. Here he presents a picture of himself for future generations:

Petrarch, often called the father of humanism, wears the laurel wreath crown that proclaims him poet laureate of Rome.

> *You may perhaps have heard something about me—although it is doubtful that my poor little name may travel far in space and time. Still, you may by chance want to know what sort of man I was. . . .*
>
> *In my youth I was blessed with an active, agile body, though not particularly strong. I can't boast of being handsome, but in my greener years I made a good impression. I had a fine complexion, between light and dark, ardent eyes, and a vision that was for many years very sharp. (But it failed me unexpectedly when I was over sixty, so that I was forced reluctantly to the use of spectacles.) . . .*
>
> *I devoted myself, though not exclusively, to the study of ancient times, since I always disliked our own period; so that, if it hadn't been for the love of those dear to me, I should have preferred being born in any other age, forgetting this one; and I always tried to transport myself mentally to other times.*

the Byzantine Empire. In 1453, the Ottoman Turks captured Constantinople. Many Byzantine scholars fleeing the city escaped to Italy, bearing precious texts. Some set themselves up in their new home as teachers, helping Italian scholars learn about the culture, language, and writings of ancient Greece.

"The Italian humanists," says historian John Hale, "were discovering their own ancestors, finding buried treasure in their own house." Each newly found Greek or Latin text was greeted with burning excitement. Each was copied and distributed, endlessly read and passionately debated. Nowhere were the discussions livelier and the consequences more dramatic than in busy, tumultuous Florence.

"New Romans" in Florence

In 1375, Coluccio Salutati was elected chancellor of Florence—the government secretary responsible for writing public documents and letters to foreign powers. Salutati was a great admirer of Petrarch and the new learning. In the 1390s, when the armies of Milan threatened Florence, the chancellor issued a series of patriotic letters rallying Florentines to their city's defense. Written in elegant Latin and inspired by ancient Roman ideals of duty and liberty, his writings were so powerful that the duke of Milan complained that a letter by Salutati was worth more than a thousand cavalry. In 1402, the duke died and Milan gave up its attack. Crediting their survival to the chancellor's inspiring letters and the lessons of the ancients, the people of Florence embraced the new learning.

In his writings, Salutati presented a portrait of the ideal man. Like the worthy citizens of ancient Rome, this "new Roman" was both scholar and statesman. Educated in a wide range of subjects, he recognized his duty to work tirelessly for the public good. The circle of humanists who met in the chancellor's house, which included not only teachers and scholars but merchants, bankers, and nobles, debated and acted on these ideas. Wealthy Florentine humanists financed the work of the scholars who hunted out ancient manuscripts. Some built up fine libraries of rare books, arranged for translations, and founded schools. Others fulfilled their citizenship duties by paying for public building projects and commissioning works of art.

After Salutati's death in 1406, a new generation of humanists continued to develop and spread his ideas. Chancellors encouraged the study

Members of the Platonic Academy attend a "birthday party" for the ancient Greek philosopher Plato at Lorenzo de' Medici's country estate in 1474. The academy—an informal group of intellectuals and artists who met to study and discuss Greek philosophy—became the center of the new philosophy known as humanism.

of the classics and held up Florence as a model of culture and enlightenment. Merchants and bankers used their wealth to attract scholars from all over Italy to Florence. The city's leading families—especially the Medici—turned their palaces and estates into centers of humanist culture. Cosimo de' Medici collected thousands of rare hand-copied books and hired the young Florentine scholar Marsilio Ficino to translate the complete works of Plato from Greek into Latin, a tremendous task that took eighteen years to complete. Cosimo also formed the Platonic Academy—an informal circle of humanists who met from time to time at the Medicis' country estate to study ancient Greek philosophy and discuss the latest ideas. Under his son Lorenzo de'

Medici, the Platonic Academy developed into the heart of humanist study and thought.

By the fifteenth century, humanism was the driving force in Florentine society. More than a philosophy, it had become a way of life, touching and transforming education, government and politics, religion, and the arts.

"A Free World of Free Spirits"

The humanists believed that they were destined to restore the glory of ancient Greece and Rome. Creating that new golden age required a whole new approach to education. With the rise of the middle class, many parents had begun sending their children to school. At first, education was a dull affair. Teachers focused mainly on practical skills such as writing and math; after all, the purpose of education was to learn the skills needed for work. Reading from dull medieval textbooks, students learned by memorizing and reciting rules and formulas.

Humanist educators had a different idea. They believed that education was worthwhile in itself, not simply as a tool for succeeding in business or trade. The aim of these teachers was to train students not just for a job but for life. Inspired by the ancient Romans, they endeavored to shape well-rounded, virtuous individuals who would contribute to the good of society. Humanist lessons were based in the liberal arts—a broad course of study that might include grammar, poetry, history, philosophy, music, literature, art, science, and rhetoric (the art of persuasive speech and writing). "The liberal arts," explained Leonardo Bruni, Florentine chancellor after Salutati, "liberate man and make him master of himself in a free world of free spirits."

In humanist schools, the dry medieval textbooks were replaced by new texts featuring Plato, Virgil, and other classical writers and philosophers. Now, while they studied their lessons, children could absorb the best of the ancient world. Many schools in Italy buzzed with the excitement of the new learning. At the Casa Giocosa, or "House of Fun," in the northern city of Mantua, lessons were tailored to the needs of each student. "Not everyone is good at everything," explained teacher Vittorino da Feltre, "but to each, nature . . . has assigned his task." Taking in the children of poor families to educate alongside those of nobles, Vittorino

Discipline was more relaxed in humanist schools than in the traditional houses of learning—although most teachers probably weren't as permissive as this patient tutor. His students are the children of Ludovico Sforza, a powerful duke who seized control of Milan in 1494 and was known for both his cold-bloodedness and his love of the arts.

created a very modern program that mixed classes in gymnastics and exercise with lessons on Latin grammar and ancient history.

Vittorino and other humanist teachers encouraged children to think and question. They taught their students that it was every individual's duty to strive for excellence. A person's place in life was not necessarily dictated by God's will; instead, human beings could control their own destiny, improve themselves, rise to greatness. "With freedom of choice and with honor," wrote humanist scholar Giovanni Pico della Mirandola, "you may fashion yourself in whatever shape you shall prefer."

Reshaping the World

Many of the children of nobles and princes and city leaders, of merchants and bankers and skilled workers, were educated in Italian humanist schools. The new system of education led them to change the world.

Generations shaped by the new learning headed the governments of Florence, Mantua, and other city-states. These humanist rulers brought philosophers, teachers, writers, poets, musicians, artists, and architects to their estates and courts. The powerful Sforza family of Milan made that city-state a center of Greek and Latin study, and the dukes of Ferrara were generous patrons of art, poetry, music, and drama. Duke Federigo of Urbino, educated at Vittorino's school in Mantua, spent a fortune on ancient manuscripts and modern paintings. Federigo's household included five scholars who read aloud from Roman texts during meals, and he practiced the humanist ideal of public service by rescuing shopkeepers from debt and giving grain to the poor.

In the lower levels of government, humanists served as secretaries and advisers to popes, princes, and leading families. Others became ambassadors who represented their city-states to foreign powers, helping to carry the spirit of humanism throughout Italy and the rest of Europe.

Humanism and Faith

The freethinking spirit of humanism, with its belief in the unlimited potential of the individual, gave many people the confidence to question long-standing ideas. Some, like Galileo and Martin Luther, challenged the teachings and practices of the church. One early humanist who especially disturbed church leaders was Lorenzo Valla, another graduate of Vittorino's school in Mantua. In 1440, using his extensive knowledge of Latin and history, Valla proved that the Donation of Constantine—a document that supposedly gave the pope the right to rule the western territories of the ancient Roman Empire—was a fake. The church denounced Valla as a heretic and forced him to flee for his life. But the scholar was not questioning God or religion, only the pope's right to meddle in politics. Like most humanists, Valla was a devout Catholic who constantly searched for a harmony between classical ideals and the Christian faith.

Renaissance writers and artists also worked to balance their faith and their philosophy. Studying the Greek and Roman cultures, they rediscovered classical ideals, styles, and techniques, and used them to create some of the world's greatest works of literature and art. Their works glorified God and carried the message of faith to a people whose lives revolved around religion. But they also reflected the humanist emphasis on human beings and their world.

Writers experimented with new ideas and new forms of literature, presenting everyday experiences in the common language of the vernacular. Painters and sculptors studied the world around them and captured it in beautifully realistic, emotionally powerful art. To these artists and to the patrons who commissioned palaces and monuments, personal portraits and scenes from ancient history, art existed not only to serve God but to mirror the beauty and wonders of the real world. A beautiful work of art was worthwhile not because it served a purpose, but in itself. That belief, like so many other ideas and achievements of the Italian Renaissance, would survive to inspire and shape the world we live in today.

MACHIAVELLI'S *PRINCE*

A student of humanism, Niccolò Machiavelli served in the government of Florence during years of foreign invasions and war among the city-states. When he lost his job in 1512, Machiavelli retired to his country estate to study history and write on politics. In *The Prince,* he presented a practical but gloomy assessment of the qualities a ruler needs to succeed in a brutal, imperfect world. Rejecting the humanist belief in the basic goodness of humanity, Machiavelli describes his ideal prince as a ruthless dictator who knows that any means—force, dishonesty, cruelty—are acceptable as long as they keep the ruler in power and bring peace and order to the city-state:

> It is necessary for a prince wishing to hold his own to know how to do wrong, and to make use of it or not according to necessity. . . .
>
> Therefore a prince, so long as he keeps his subjects united and loyal, ought not to mind the reproach [accusation] of cruelty. . . .
>
> Upon this a question arises: whether it be better to be loved than feared or feared than loved? It may be answered that one should wish

Niccolò Machiavelli is remembered today mainly for the ruthless view of politics he presented in The Prince. *The Florentine statesman and philosopher also wrote poems and plays (including one popular comedy), as well as essays in support of democratic principles.*

to be both, but, because it is difficult to unite them in one person, it is much safer to be feared than loved. . . .

A wise lord cannot, nor ought he to, keep faith [his promises] when such observance may be turned against him, and when the reasons that caused him to pledge it exist no longer. If men were entirely good this precept [rule] would not hold, but because they are bad, and will not keep faith with you, you too are not bound to observe it with them. . . .

But it is necessary to know well how to disguise this characteristic, and to be a great pretender and dissembler [faker]; and men are so simple . . . that he who seeks to deceive will always find someone who will allow himself to be deceived.

CHAPTER FIVE

OUR RENAISSANCE WORLD

No single date or event marked the end of the Italian Renaissance. Sometime in the late sixteenth century, it simply began to fade away.

Following the sack of Rome in 1527, Spain gained control of all the large city-states except Venice. In that great city on the sea, Renaissance culture continued to flourish for another half century. But Italy's star was falling. With Christopher Columbus's voyages across the Atlantic, Spain had opened up new trade routes to the Americas. Portugal controlled rich sea routes to Asia and Africa. Gradually these two nations replaced the Italian city-states as centers of trade and wealth.

Changes within the Catholic Church also contributed to the end of the Renaissance in Italy. In the mid-1500s, after Martin Luther launched the Protestant Reformation, the church responded with its own reform movement. This Catholic Reformation, or Counter-Reformation, brought some much-needed changes. For example, it ended the sale of high-ranking positions in the church and tightened controls over the education and behavior of local priests. But the Counter-Reformation also cracked down on independent thought. The Inquisition—a religious court formed in the thirteenth century to combat heresy—came under the control of the popes in Rome and stepped up its activities. Freethinkers such as Galileo were dragged before the Inquisition and forced to renounce their beliefs. A few were burned at the stake. The threat of the Inquisition, along with the decline of the power and independence of the city-states, stifled the spirit of learning and discovery in Italy.

Across the Alps

Even as the spirit of the Renaissance died out in Italy, it was finding new life in the rest of Europe. Since the early 1300s, Italian traders, bankers, artists, and scholars had been carrying Renaissance ideas across the Alps, to northern and western Europe. Invading armies from France, Spain, and

Lucas Cranach the Elder of Germany painted these three Saxon Princesses in 1535. A friend of Martin Luther, the German Renaissance artist also painted many Protestant leaders and biblical scenes that expressed the ideas and spirit of the Reformation.

other powers also spread the news of the glorious Renaissance culture. Soon scholars from all over Europe were traveling to Italy. Writers came to pore through the classical texts in Italian libraries. Educators studied under humanist teachers, absorbing their new teaching methods. Artists and architects marveled at ancient Roman works of art and the styles and techniques of Italian Renaissance masters. Returning home, these travelers interpreted the knowledge they had gained in the light of their own cultures, exploring ever wider worlds of thought and expression.

61

In Flanders, a region in parts of France, Belgium, and the Netherlands, artists experimented with new oil-painting techniques, creating highly realistic, boldly colored paintings. Composers developed new forms of music, including counterpoint (combining voices in harmony). Flemish painters and composers traveled to Italy, sharing their new ideas and in turn being influenced by Italian paintings and popular songs.

Flemish painter Quentin Massys was influenced by Italian and German Renaissance art, especially the works of Leonardo da Vinci and Albrecht Dürer. Massys painted this portrait of the Dutch humanist Erasmus in 1517.

Elsewhere in the Netherlands, Desiderius Erasmus became one of the most famous humanists of the sixteenth century. A priest who traveled and taught throughout Europe, Erasmus often wrote about religion and the need for reform within the church. His books were best-sellers, making him the first author ever to support himself solely from the sale of his writings.

One of Germany's most important Renaissance figures was the artist Albrecht Dürer. In the late 1400s, Dürer spent two years in Venice, studying art, perspective, and human anatomy. Writing to a friend, he noted that, while in Germany a painter was considered a lowly craftsman, in Italy he was celebrated as a glorious creator. In time, Dürer's paintings, which combined Italian techniques with German traditions, earned him that same respect and renown. But his greatest contributions were his advances in the art of woodcuts and engravings. Using the techniques he developed, printers were able to produce more detailed, expressive reproductions of art for books.

Giants, Windmills, and Tempests

In France, the Renaissance culture flowered in the early 1500s, under King Francis I. The French king invited Italian artists including Leonardo da Vinci to court and sponsored the work of French artists, architects, and scholars. While serving as court librarian for Francis, French scholar Guillaume Budé established one of the first humanist universities, the College of France, where students received a broad education in the liberal arts.

Like Italian Renaissance writers, the French experimented with new forms of literature written in their native language. In 1532, François Rabelais began writing the first novel in the French vernacular, about a pair of giants named Gargantua and Pantagruel. Published as five books, Rabelais's work is a comic masterpiece that pokes fun at European society and the church.

Spanish writer Miguel de Cervantes Saavedra also wrote novels in the vernacular. Cervantes's famous *Don Quixote,* published in 1605, presents the adventures of a befuddled Spanish noble who sees himself as a medieval knight. Traveling across Spain with his trusty servant Sancho Panza, Don Quixote battles windmills that he thinks are giants and rescues a peasant-girl "princess." Along the way, he meets a cast of characters from many walks of life, who embody all the weaknesses and virtues of Spanish Renaissance society.

German artist Albrecht Dürer brought many of the ideas of the Italian Renaissance to northern Europe, combining them with the region's own artistic traditions. Saint Jerome in His Study *is one of Dürer's finely detailed woodcuts—prints made from designs carved into wood, used as book illustrations. Saint Jerome was a fourth-century Christian scholar.*

A CARNIVAL SONG

The Renaissance world rang with music: choirs singing at church services; bands of drummers, trumpeters, and fife players celebrating weddings, festivals, and holy days; upper-class men and women showing off their skills at the harpsichord or lute. The musicians of Renaissance Italy invented the harpsichord and violin. They developed the madrigal (a kind of vocal music with parts for several voices) and printed the first musical scores showing words and notes together. But the leading musicians of the Renaissance came from northern Europe. English, French, and Flemish composers experimented with new, richer forms of music featuring two or more melodies played in harmony. While religious music remained popular, many of their compositions were based on nonreligious tunes, and some set the words of ancient Roman or modern Renaissance poets to music.

Lorenzo de' Medici was an accomplished poet who wrote this song as a young man already looking ahead to a lifetime of hard work and public service:

Fair is youth and void of sorrow;
But it hourly flies away.
Youths and maids, enjoy today;
Nought ye know about tomorrow. . . .

Midas treads a [weary] measure:
All he touches turns to gold:
If there be no taste of pleasure,
What's the use of wealth untold?
What's the joy his fingers hold,
When he's forced to thirst for aye
* [always]?*
Youths and maids, enjoy today;
Nought ye know about tomorrow.

Listen well to what we're saying;
Of tomorrow have no care!
Young and old together playing,
Boys and girls, be blithe [lighthearted]
* as air!*
Every sorry thought forswear [reject]!
Keep perpetual holiday.
Youths and maid, enjoy today;
Nought ye know about tomorrow.

Ladies and gay lovers young!
Long live Bacchus [god of wine],
* live Desire!*
Dance and play; let songs be sung;
Let sweet love your bosoms fire;
In the future come what may!
Youths and maids, enjoy today!
Nought ye know about tomorrow.

The first great vernacular writer in English was Geoffrey Chaucer, whose masterpiece was *The Canterbury Tales*, written in the late 1300s. In this long poem, a group of pilgrims on their way to a religious shrine pass the time by telling stories. Chaucer's tales range from highly moral to bawdy, and his characters may be noble or common, kindly or evil.

The English Renaissance really took off in the late 1500s, during the reign of Queen Elizabeth I. In the Elizabethan period, English writers opened up new worlds of literature, with brilliant poetry by Sir Walter Raleigh and Edmund Spenser as well as groundbreaking essays on experimental science by Sir Francis Bacon. Especially exciting were the vivid, action-packed plays by Christopher Marlowe, Ben Jonson, and, greatest of them all, William Shakespeare. A number of Shakespeare's plays were based on classical or Italian stories. *Romeo and Juliet* tells the tragic tale of two young lovers from battling families in the northern Italian city of Verona. In *The Tempest,* warring nobles from Milan are shipwrecked and work out their differences on a mysterious island inhabited by ancient Roman spirits.

Across the Ages

From Florence to the rest of Italy, from Italy to the rest of Europe, from Europe to the Americas—the Italian Renaissance spread and took root, leaving its lasting mark on the whole Western world. To many historians, the Renaissance was the beginning of the modern age. Today we can still see its legacy in our politics and economy, society and culture.

Renaissance humanist ideals live on in our modern-day belief in the value of public service and the duty of elected officials to serve the interests of the people they represent. Renaissance Italians also shaped modern diplomacy by sending the first ambassadors to live in other cities and countries. In times of war and competition among the city-states, it was important to have representatives abroad who were trained in the art of rhetoric. Early ambassadors negotiated trade agreements and peace treaties and sent home reports on foreign politics and leaders. Our modern diplomats do the same job. Today's politicians also use rhetoric to seek votes and win support for their ideas and policies. When they go too far, adopting the ideas expressed by Machiavelli in *The Prince*—any action that keeps a leader in power is acceptable—we call them "Machiavellian."

The merchants and bankers of the Italian Renaissance invented many practices that have become part of our modern economy. They gave loans, sold insurance, and offered credit, allowing customers to "buy now and pay later." The middle class rose in importance and influence throughout Europe during the Renaissance, transforming the economy and society. For the first time, the average man (or, in rare instances, woman) had a chance to work his way up the social ladder through his own efforts in education, business, and trade.

Modern science was built on the foundations of Renaissance thought. The scholars who used observation and experiments to peer into the mysteries of the natural world developed a process known today as the scientific method. When the Renaissance ended in the mid-seventeenth century, many important scientific discoveries still lay ahead: causes and cures for diseases, the physical laws governing the universe, the technology behind rockets and space travel. All these achievements would be based on the eager, inquiring spirit of science born in the Italian Renaissance.

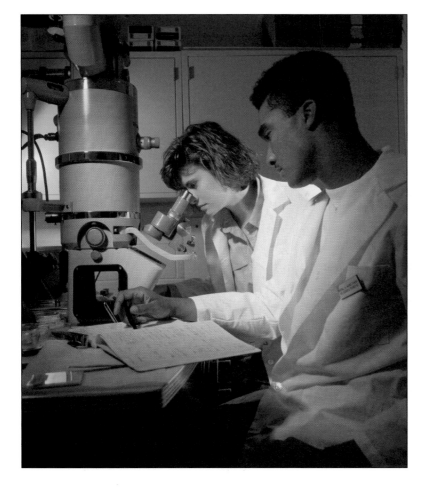

These modern science students owe a debt to the Renaissance scholars who used firsthand observation and experiments to seek a deeper understanding of the natural world.

The Living Renaissance

Today people from all over the world visit Florence, Rome, and Venice to marvel at the wonders of art and architecture created by the Renaissance masters. Art students still learn the techniques of perspective and proportion developed by Brunelleschi. They follow in the footsteps of Leonardo and Michelangelo when they study nature and human anatomy to learn how to represent not just objects and figures but feelings and ideas.

But the Renaissance artists and their patrons did more than create magnificent, inventive works that continue to delight and inspire us today. They also changed the way people thought about art. From Lorenzo de' Medici, Michelangelo, and other freethinkers, we have inherited the idea of "art for art's sake": a beautiful work of art can be appreciated not because it has a practical purpose, but simply because it is beautiful.

Italian Renaissance writers changed the world of literature, with the development of vernacular writing. Enriched with elements from Latin and Greek, their "everyday" Italian allowed writers to express ideas in elegant, flowing prose that could be read not only by the well educated but by ordinary people, too. The poems, novels, essays, and plays of Renaissance France, Spain, and England—along with those of our modern world—all owe a debt to Petrarch, Boccaccio, and the other great Italian vernacular writers.

Many of the outstanding writers, artists, and scholars of Renaissance Italy were educated by humanist teachers. The humanist system of education became the model for schools throughout Europe and the American colonies. Today, in schools and universities across the Western world, young people study many of the same subjects taught in Italian humanist schools: grammar, literature, rhetoric, history, math, science, music, art. Their teachers strive to turn out well-rounded individuals who will become good and useful members of society. They try to inspire their students with an ideal that was central to humanism: with hard work and dedication, you can be anything you want to be.

That belief may be one of the most important legacies of the Italian Renaissance. After all, the Renaissance began with a new way of looking at the world. Scholars, artists, and scientists began to search for truth through their own experiences—to question, observe, experiment, and draw their own conclusions. They learned to trust in their unique talents

The stories of Giovanni Boccaccio—especially the witty and colorful Decameron—*became a model for Italian Renaissance writings. This portrait of Boccaccio is part of a fresco showing famous men and women that was painted by fifteenth-century Florentine artist Andrea del Castagno.*

and abilities, and to strive for excellence. Today, when we plant a seed to learn how plants grow, keep a diary of our thoughts and dreams, or admire the beautiful graphics in a computer game, we are all children of the Italian Renaissance.

The Italian Renaissance: A Time Line

Ottoman Turks capture Constantinople **1453**

Johannes Gutenberg invents the printing press **1450**

Cosimo de' Medici opens Europe's first public library, in Florence **1444**

Lorenzo Valla proves the Donation of Constantine a forgery **1440**

Brunelleschi completes the dome of the cathedral of Florence **1436**

Medici family gains control of the government of Florence **1434**

Donatello begins work on bronze statue of *David* **1430**

Wars between Florence and Naples **1408–1414**

Florence conquers Pisa **1406**

Milan at war with Florence **1390–1402**

Popolo grasso regain power in Florence; **1382**
Albizzi family dominates the government

Common workers and *popolo minuto* **1378**
revolt against *popolo grasso* in Florence

1353 Giovanni Boccaccio completes the *Decameron*

1347–1351 Black Death sweeps Europe

1341 Petrarch crowned poet laureate in Rome

1339 First of four major famines strikes Italy and much of Europe

1302 Dante Alighieri banished from Florence; begins writing *The Divine Comedy*

1500	**1550**	**1600**

Galileo publishes *Dialogue Concerning the Two Chief World Systems* **1632**

1543 Catholic Church bans Copernicus's book on the solar system

1527 Sack of Rome; end of High Renaissance

1517 Martin Luther's Ninety-five Theses starts the Protestant Reformation

1513 Giovanni de' Medici becomes Pope Leo X;
Niccolò Macchiavelli writes *The Prince*

1508 Michelangelo begins the ceiling of the Sistine Chapel; Raphael
paints papal apartments in the Vatican Palace

1504 Michelangelo completes statue of *David*

1495 Leonardo da Vinci paints *The Last Supper;* beginning of High Renaissance

1494 King Charles VIII of France invades Italy

1492 Death of Lorenzo de' Medici

1480 Botticelli paints *Birth of Venus*

1478 Pazzi family and Pope Sixtus IV fail in attempt to overthrow the Medicis

1469 Lorenzo de' Medici becomes unofficial ruler of Florence

GLOSSARY

bishop: an official in the Catholic Church, ranking above a priest

Black Death: a form of bubonic plague that took many lives in Europe and Asia during the fourteenth century; caused by bacteria, the plague was spread by fleas that bit infected rats and then bit humans

cardinal: an important official in the Catholic Church, ranking just below the pope

city-state: an independent political unit made up of a governing city and the land surrounding it

classical: relating to the ancient Greeks and Romans

convent: a place where nuns—female members of a religious community—live together, apart from the world

Crusades: a series of wars waged by European Christians between the eleventh and thirteenth centuries to gain control of Muslim-ruled Jerusalem and other areas in the Middle East

diplomacy: the practice of handling negotiations and agreements between foreign powers

Donation of Constantine: a document, supposedly written in the days of the Roman emperor Constantine, that gave the popes the legal right to control territories of the ancient Roman Empire; in 1440, Italian humanist Lorenzo Valla proved that the document was a forgery, written at a later time

Flemish: from Flanders, a historic region in northern Europe, which included parts of France, Belgium, and the Netherlands

fresco: a wall painting made on freshly spread plaster

harpsichord: a musical instrument popular in the sixteenth through nineteenth centuries, which looks like a small piano but usually has two keyboards

heretic: a person accused of heresy, or expressing opinions contrary to the official teachings of the Catholic Church

Holy Land: another name for Palestine, the historic region in the Middle East that includes Jerusalem and other places holy to Jews, Christians, and Muslims

interest: in banking, money that a borrower pays to a lender in return for the use of the borrowed money

liberal arts: studies that are meant to develop general knowledge, thinking, and reasoning rather than simply preparing the student for a particular job

lute: a stringed instrument something like a guitar, with a large pear-shaped body and bent neck

mercenary: a soldier who is hired to fight in a foreign army and serves only for the pay

Middle Ages: the time period in European history from the fall of Rome in 476 to the beginning of the Renaissance in the fourteenth century

monk: a man who is a member of a religious order and lives apart from the world in a monastery

naturalism: a style of art in which living creatures and the natural world are portrayed as accurately and realistically as possible

patron: a wealthy person who gives money to help support an artist, a writer, or a cause

perspective: a technique based on mathematical rules that is used to give depth to paintings and make objects appear three-dimensional; far-away objects are shown smaller than nearby ones, and lines get closer together as they move toward a "vanishing point" in the distance

proportion: the balanced arrangement of different parts of a building or other object

purgatory: according to Catholic teachings, a "middle" place where the souls of those who are destined for heaven but die with unrepented sins are sent to be punished and purified

relics: items believed to be the physical remains of saints (such as a bone) or something associated with them (a scrap of clothing or a splinter from the cross on which Jesus was crucified), which are regarded with respect and devotion

Renaissance: the cultural movement that spread throughout Europe from roughly the fourteenth to seventeenth centuries, laying the foundation for the politics, science, philosophy, and art of the modern Western world

scribe: a person who copies out letters, books, and other writings by hand

Signoria (seen-YAWR-ee-uh): the most important governing body in Renaissance Florence, made up of nine officials, each elected to serve for two months

vernacular: the everyday language of a particular region or country

FOR FURTHER READING

Clare, John D., ed. *Italian Renaissance*. San Diego: Harcourt Brace, 1995.

Day, Nancy. *Your Travel Guide to Renaissance Europe*. Minneapolis: Runestone Press, 2001.

Hinds, Kathryn. *Venice and Its Merchant Empire*. Cultures of the Past series. New York: Marshall Cavendish, 2001.

January, Brendan. *Science in the Renaissance*. New York: Franklin Watts, 1999.

Langley, Andrew. *Leonardo and His Times*. New York: Dorling Kindersley, 2000.

Lyon, Sue, ed. *The Italian Renaissance*. New York: Marshall Cavendish, 1989.

MacDonald, Fiona. *The World in the Time of Leonardo da Vinci*. Parsippany, NJ: Dillon Press, 1998.

Milande, Véronique. *Michelangelo and His Times*. New York: Henry Holt, 1996.

Morley, Jacqueline, and Mark Peppé. *A Renaissance Town*. New York: Peter Bedrick, 1996.

Netzley, Patricia D. *Life during the Renaissance*. San Diego: Lucent, 1998.

Osman, Karen. *The Italian Renaissance*. San Diego: Lucent, 1996.

Spence, David. *Michelangelo and the Renaissance*. Hauppauge, NY: Barron's Educational Series, 1997.

Walker, Paul Robert. *The Italian Renaissance*. New York: Facts on File, 1995.

ON-LINE INFORMATION*

"Exploring Leonardo" at http://www.mos.org/sln/Leonardo

> This interactive resource for teachers and students explores the life and times of Renaissance scientist, inventor, and artist Leonardo da Vinci. © 1997 Museum of Science, Boston.

"The Italian Renaissance Art Project" at http://irap.wonsaponatime.net

> View biographical information and "artistic samples" from Italian Renaissance artists Leonardo da Vinci, Michelangelo, Raphael, Botticelli, Giotto, and Fra Angelico.

"The Italian Renaissance of the 15th Century" at

> http://www.best.com/~natalew/zItalyRen.html

> View art by selected fifteenth-century Italian painters, sculptors, and architects. © 1999, 2000 Natale Williams.

"A Journey through the Renaissance" at

> http://library.thinkquest.org/C005356

> Excellent animation and sound effects take you through the key historical events in Italy and the rest of Europe, with detours to explore Renaissance art, music, and science. This site was created for the ThinkQuest 2000 Internet Challenge by three high school students.

"The Rebirth of Europe: Renaissance" at

> http://library.thinkquest.org/C006522

> Well-written, encyclopedia-style articles examine Renaissance art, literature, science and technology, exploration and trade, religion, politics, and daily life. © 2000 C006522 ThinkQuest team.

*Websites change from time to time. For additional on-line information, check with the media specialist at your local library.

BIBLIOGRAPHY

Atchity, Kenneth J., ed. *The Renaissance Reader.* New York: HarperCollins, 1996.

Boccaccio, Giovanni. *The Decameron of Giovanni Boccaccio.* Translated by John Payne. New York: Walter J. Black, 1972.

Brucker, Gene Adam. *Florence: The Golden Age, 1138–1737.* New York: Abbeville Press, 1984.

———. *Renaissance Florence.* Berkeley: University of California Press, 1983.

The Catholic Encyclopedia at http://www.newadvent.org/cathen ©1998 by Robert Appleton Company, on-line edition © 2001 by Kevin Knight.

Corrick, James A. *The Renaissance.* San Diego: Lucent, 1998.

Guicciardini, Francesco. *History of Italy and History of Florence.* Translated by Cecil Grayson. New York: Washington Square Press, 1964.

King, Margaret L. *Women of the Renaissance.* Chicago: University of Chicago Press, 1991.

Leonardo da Vinci. *The Notebooks of Leonardo da Vinci.* Edited by Jean Paul Richter. Vol. 1. New York: Dover, 1972.

Machiavelli, Niccolò. *The Prince.* Translated by W. K. Marriott. New York: Alfred A. Knopf, 1992.

Martinelli, Giuseppe, ed. *The World of Renaissance Florence.* London: MacDonald, 1968.

Mee, Charles L., Jr. *The Horizon Book of Daily Life in Renaissance Italy.* New York: American Heritage, 1975.

———. *Lorenzo de' Medici and The Renaissance.* New York: American Heritage, 1969.

Ross, James Bruce, and Mary Martin McLaughlin, eds. *The Portable Renaissance Reader.* New York: Penguin Books, 1981.

Thompson, Stephen P., ed. *The Renaissance.* San Diego: Greenhaven Press, 2000.

INDEX

Page numbers for illustrations are in boldface

ABOUT THE AUTHOR

Virginia Schomp has written dozens of books for young readers, including two other titles in the CULTURES OF THE PAST series, *Japan in the Days of the Samurai* and *The Ancient Greeks*. When she's not busy writing, she enjoys reading, watching old movies, singing in a choir, gardening, hiking, and boating. Ms. Schomp lives in the Catskill Mountain region of New York with her husband, Richard, and their son, Chip.